Original title:
A Laughter of Leaves

Copyright © 2025 Creative Arts Management OÜ
All rights reserved.

Author: Nash Everly
ISBN HARDBACK: 978-1-80567-394-1
ISBN PAPERBACK: 978-1-80567-693-5

The Humor in Hues

When autumn paints with vibrant shades,
The trees wear chuckles, lighten our days.
Scarlet whispers and golden grins,
Each rustle hints at the fun within.

Squirrels giggle, taking their flight,
As leaves dance boldly, a funny sight.
Nature's palette, a playful tease,
Swirling joy on a gentle breeze.

Chortles in the Canopy

In the boughs above, the branches sway,
Tickling each leaf in a merry ballet.
With every gust, a giggle grows,
As sunlight winks and mischief flows.

Creaking limbs share secrets bright,
A symphony of humor, pure delight.
The acorns laugh, they tumble down,
As nature's jesters wear their crown.

The Symphony of Swirling Colors

A vibrant orchestra sings so sweet,
With rustling leaves, a rhythmic beat.
Colors clash in a playful parade,
Creating laughter, in nature's charade.

The jade and amber, they play tag,
In this wild dance, there's no room to lag.
Each swirling leaf, a note of glee,
In the concert of trees, come dance with me.

Giggles in the Gales

Through whispering winds, the leaves do jest,
Spinning tales of fun, they're truly blessed.
A breezy hug, a ticklish pass,
Time to snicker, watching the grass.

The clouds join in with a chuckle or two,
As sunlight beams down, a laughing hue.
Each gust carries joy like a song,
Reminding us all that we belong.

Joyful Undertones in the Orchard

In the orchard, fruits collide,
Where bananas start to slide.
Apples giggle, plums joke around,
With each rustle, humor is found.

The sunbeams tickle branches high,
As pears engage in a playful spy.
Grapes bounce on their tiny feet,
Spreading laughter, oh what a treat!

Through the fields, a breeze will play,
Whispering tales of a funny day.
Cherries blush in a merry dance,
In this orchard, joy takes a chance.

With every rustle, a chuckle near,
In this haven, there's nothing to fear.
Laughter mingles with the fruit's sweet scent,
As nature's humor is freely spent.

The Cheery Charade of Colors

In the forest, colors collide,
Where greens wear stripes, and yellows abide.
A purple leaf takes a silly bow,
While orange tones laugh—what a show!

The sun-warmed hues hold a grand parade,
As tints of joy serenely invade.
Each shade winks in playful delight,
Turning the day into colorful light.

Rustling whispers share a prank,
While azure shades spill laughter's rank.
Something strange in each hue portrayed,
In this charade, no shade is afraid.

As colors giggle under the bright,
Orchards echo with pure delight.
With their joyful antics on display,
The cheery charade rules the day!

Leaves that Chuckle

Leaves that chuckle in the breeze,
Dancing lightly among the trees.
Each flutter brings a twist of fate,
In nature's humor, they congregate.

Breezes giggle, pushing high,
While branches sway and branches fly.
A rustling symphony takes the stage,
In the forest, by laughter, they engage.

Crickets join with a chirp and cheer,
As the leaves whisper jokes to ear.
Their mirthful secrets fill the day,
In every shade, they play and sway.

With whispers shared among the groves,
The chortling leaves tell all their oaths.
In each little turn, joy is found,
As nature spins laughter all around.

Smiles on the Branches

Breezy giggles sway and dance,
The branches chuckle, take a chance.
A rustle here, a whisper there,
Nature's jest, light as the air.

Squirrels prance with cheeky glee,
Swinging high from tree to tree.
A leaf drops down, a playful tease,
Tickling toes in the summer breeze.

Whimsy in the Wilderness

The bushes hum a silly song,
As critters join, they can't go wrong.
Branches twist, a game of hide,
Who can find the fox with pride?

Dancing daisies spin around,
While bumblebees make funny sounds.
A toad jumps up, in pure delight,
As shadows stretch in fading light.

The Bloom of Banter

Petals chatter in the sun,
With every breeze, they mumble fun.
A ladybug slips, oh what a sight,
Rolling down, a pure delight.

The flowers giggle, colors bright,
Painting laughter in daylight.
A butterfly winks, a playful bluff,
As bees buzz by, they can't get enough.

Playful Patterns Above

Clouds toss jokes from high above,
Raindrops dance, they're in love.
The sun peeks through with a smirk,
Lighting up the playful work.

Windy whispers tickle trees,
As shadows stretch, the world agrees.
A kite soars with vibrant cheer,
Waving down to all who hear.

Whispers in the Wind

The breeze tells jokes with a playful twirl,
As branches sway in a spiral swirl.
Tickles of air dance 'round the trees,
Carrying chuckles with each gentle breeze.

Squirrels giggle, a jolly sight,
As they leap and bound in pure delight.
The rustle of leaves joins in the cheer,
A chorus of fun that's ever so clear.

The Chortle of Canopies

High above, the leaves share tales,
Of silly winds and dramatic gales.
Each flap and flutter, a burst of fun,
A canopy comedy under the sun.

Branches bend with a merry shake,
While shadows dance and pranks they make.
With every sway, a giggle takes flight,
Brightening the woods, a pure delight.

Giggles Beneath the Branches

Rustling whispers tickle the ground,
Where tiny critters prance all around.
Beneath the branches, laughter explodes,
In the playful paths where nature goads.

A toadstool party, giggles abound,
With playful mushrooms gathering around.
The grass joins in, a green glee spree,
Echoing joys of wild jubilee.

Mirth in the Meadow

Fields of gold with a cheeky grin,
Flowers sway as the laughter begins.
Bumblebees buzz with a humdrum cheer,
While daisies dance, drawing all near.

Each blade of grass conducts a tune,
As sunlight filters through afternoon.
The meadow echoes a jovial sound,
Where spirits soar and joy's unbound.

Whimsy Among the Woods

Trees wear hats of sunny gold,
Their branches dance, a tale untold.
Squirrels giggle, chasing dreams,
While sunlight winks, or so it seems.

Breezes tickle mossy floors,
Flipping leaves like playful doors.
A rabbit hops in silly shoes,
Spreading joy with every snooze.

Mushrooms chuckle at the ground,
As shadows paint the world around.
A cheeky fox in jester's guise,
Makes even owls roll their eyes.

In this forest, silly and bold,
Every giggle, a story told.
Nature's quirks in colors bright,
Dancing through the day and night.

Cackles in the Clearing

In the glade where shadows play,
Laughter blooms in wild display.
Ducks in bow ties, strut with pride,
While daisies gossip, side by side.

Bumblebees play tag with air,
A nimble sprite just stops to stare.
Frogs in chorus sing with glee,
Each croak a note of jubilee.

Whirling leaves like confetti fly,
Butterflies spin, oh my, oh my!
An acorn drops with quite a thud,
Causing giggles from the mud.

In the clearing, mirth takes flight,
Nature's jesters spark delight.
Every branch a tale to share,
In this realm of playful air.

Humor of the Harvest

Pumpkins grin with silly smiles,
While corn stalks dance in funny styles.
A scarecrow cracks a cheesy joke,
Causing crows to laugh and choke.

Apple trees, a prankster's dream,
Dangle fruit that giggles and gleams.
The winds whisper tales of cheer,
As nature's chorus draws us near.

Squirrels stash their acorn loot,
While rabbits jiggle, legs astute.
Harvest moons break into song,
In this field where we belong.

Laughter ripens on the vine,
Each moment shared is pure divine.
The humor of the earth so bright,
Fills our hearts with pure delight.

A Mirthful Arbor

Underneath the leafy dome,
Trees share secrets of their home.
A nimble squirrel, doing flips,
Leaves giggle with the funny quips.

Branches sway in rhythmic glee,
A woodland party, wild and free.
Birds exchange their playful jests,
As sunlight peeks and smiles the best.

Bubbles form in puddles clear,
Frog musicians lend their cheer.
In every rustle, secrets hide,
Nature's laughter, a joyous ride.

The arbor hums with jolly tunes,
Waltzing stars and friendly moons.
In this garden, joy persists,
A mirthful world, too sweet to miss.

The Fragrance of Fun

In the breeze, the whispers dance,
Beneath the boughs, there's a chance,
Silly giggles from the shade,
Nature's jesters in bright parade.

Frolicsome shadows leap and twirl,
As seasons spin and colors whirl,
Squirrels jest, and branches sway,
Tickling ferns in a playful fray.

Bubbles form in fragrant air,
As laughter blooms without a care,
Jolly echoes 'neath the trees,
Nature's humor, a gentle tease.

Mirthful critters scamper wild,
Every glance, a gleeful child,
As petals chuckle, buds arise,
Joy unfolds beneath the skies.

Swaying to Nature's Tune

Dancing leaves with a wobbly jig,
They make the timid raindrops gig,
Each flutter sings a comic song,
Nature's choir, cheeky, strong.

Swaying branches bend and break,
As breezes stir a rustling wake,
Foliage chuckles, twirls and bends,
A playful show that never ends.

Whispered jests in rustling greens,
Branches tease in silly scenes,
With every gust, a hearty laugh,
Nature's art, the joyous craft.

In wild antics as shadows play,
Giggles bounce the mundane away,
With every leaf, a ticklish touch,
Oh, how nature loves to clutch.

Capering Sylvan Spirits

Beneath the trees, they prance and play,
Tiny spirits in disarray,
Chasing each other in leafy hide,
Giggling softly, spirits collide.

A tumble here, a merry roll,
Nature's jest—a raucous stroll,
Flickering shadows on the ground,
Echoes of joy and mischief abound.

With every rustle, they croon and tease,
Enchanting hearts with dappled ease,
In every nook, their laughter stays,
Capering bright through endless days.

Sprightly blooms with funny faces,
In playful whimsy, nature embraces,
A giggle shared, a twinkle bright,
Carried by breezes, pure delight.

The Serenade of Sundry Tints

In hues of amber, crimson, gold,
Leaves clang and chime, stories told,
Colors clash in a jovial hub,
Nature's band, a merry blub.

With every rustle, laughter rings,
A concert led by leafy kings,
Twilight giggles, hues unite,
A chorus sung in pure delight.

Here, purple sprouts and bluish greens,
Bounce with joy in playful scenes,
Tickled by rays of warming sun,
Sundry tints, their fun begun.

Nature smiles, her palette spread,
With colors bright as laughter wed,
In every shade, a fun embrace,
Joy entwined in time and space.

The Elation of Emeralds

In the breeze, they dance around,
Whispers tickle from the ground.
Branches shake, a giggle shared,
  Nature's joy, brightly paired.

Squirrels leap with silly glee,
Chasing shadows, wild and free.
Sunshine laughter, soft and bright,
  Emeralds twinkle in delight.

Leaves are hats for froggy friends,
  Each a joke that never ends.
  Swirling colors in a spin,
Their playful prank, a joyous grin.

  Underneath the leafy jest,
  Life finds joy, a playful fest.
Oozing smiles from every seam,
  Emerald wonders, just a dream.

Frolicsome Breezes and Blossoms

Blossoms chuckle as they bloom,
Spreading cheer, dispelling gloom.
The fluffy clouds join in the play,
Tickling flowers in a fray.

Breezes swirl, a light ballet,
Whirling petals, come what may.
Footloose dandelions hop,
Swaying lightly, then they stop.

A bee buzzes in comic flight,
Bumping blooms with sheer delight.
Giggling grass beneath our feet,
Nature's pulse, a lively beat.

With each rustle, laughter flows,
Joyful breezes softly blow.
In this garden, all can see,
Life is grand, so blissfully.

The Sunshine Within the Shades

In the shadows, warmth will play,
Tickled sunlight finds its way.
Dancing leaves in sparkly rays,
Whispering secrets, bright delays.

Sipping tea with lazy bees,
Pondering life's sweet little tease.
Laughter lingers in the shade,
Hiding tricks that light has made.

Where the sun winks through the green,
Chasing laughter, rarely seen.
Cool retreats, and giddy spins,
Make the heart do joyful wins.

Amidst the cracks and cozy nooks,
Life plays pranks with playful hooks.
In these corners, joy's parade,
Flows like water, never fade.

Purity in the Parodic Leaves

Leaves are actors on a stage,
Mimicking life, a playful page.
With silent giggles, they perform,
Nature's art, a vibrant norm.

Each rustle tells a funny tale,
Of autumn's jest and springtime's trail.
A chorus sung from trees so tall,
Echoes in the forest hall.

In their dance, the world we see,
A comedy of green debris.
Jokes exchanged in breezy shifts,
Life unfolds, and laughter lifts.

Paradox in every wave,
Leaves reveal the joy we crave.
In their flutter, truth concealed,
Nature's humor, thus revealed.

Happiness Among the Hues

In the dance of colors bright,
The leaves play tag in sunlight.
With rustles loud and giggles light,
They twirl and spin, a joyful sight.

Frolicking in the gentle breeze,
Whispers carry through the trees.
Nature's jest, a playful tease,
Bringing smiles and endless ease.

Each shade bursts forth in a cheer,
They have a party, loud and clear.
With every sway, they bring good cheer,
A canvas where our hearts come near.

In their chatter, secrets spread,
Stories of joy quietly said.
Under the sky, alight and red,
Laughter among the hues we've wed.

The Cheerful Chorus

Leaves giggle in the sunny air,
Sprouting joy without a care.
A chorus formed without compare,
Singing tunes of fun to share.

Each branch sways to the merry sound,
Dancing wildly all around.
Nature's stage, a lively ground,
As laughter swirls in every pound.

Tickling the wind with vibrant flair,
They toss their jokes, a playful dare.
In this symphony, joy lays bare,
With every rustle, joy is rare.

The forest echoes with their wise,
Witty banter, no disguise.
In painted shades beneath the skies,
A merry meeting, none denies.

Lighthearted Leaflets

Tiny leaflets chase the sun,
In a game where all can run.
Whirling, twirling, just for fun,
Their giggles bloom when day's begun.

They trade their secrets with the breeze,
Cackling in threes, like old peas.
To nature's rhythm, rapt with ease,
Dancing lightly through the trees.

Each flutter hides a playful jest,
With every gust, they jig and rest.
Life's a quest, a merry fest,
Comical tales that leaves attest.

In lighter hearts, they find their way,
Stirring laughter every day.
With colors bright, they joyfully sway,
Waving goodbye until the gray.

Radiant Revelry

Golden hues twist and shout,
In a jubilee without a doubt.
Spreading cheer, they spin about,
In the forest, laughter's clout.

Glorious rustles, joy unchained,
Ticklish breezes, love maintained.
In nature's party, none are drained,
Every chuckle, bliss proclaimed.

Lively colors bounce in glee,
Tickled whispers between each tree.
A vibrant canvas full and free,
The joy of leaves, we all agree.

In a radiant dance, they play their role,
Filling hearts, creating whole.
With every swish, they touch the soul,
Revelry's spirit, the leaves extol.

Leafy Jests

When breezes giggle, branches sway,
The trees exchange their jokes all day.
A squirrel leaps, a nut in tow,
Declaring, 'I'm the star of the show!'

With rustling whispers, secrets shared,
A dandelion's dance, so unprepared.
Oh, look at that, the petals twirl,
As butterflies join in the whirl!

Acorns chuckle, rolling down,
While mushrooms wear their cap and gown.
Snicker from roots, a ticklish tease,
Nature's humor, sure to appease!

So step into this leafy spree,
Where laughter echoes, wild and free.
Each branch a jester, each leaf a friend,
In this green world, the fun won't end!

The Playful Wind's Caress

A gust whirls by, a spark of cheer,
Tickling each leaf, making them leer.
Spinning in circles, swirls of delight,
Nature's jesters, oh what a sight!

Whispers of mischief float through the air,
As roots play poker, without a single care.
The flowers exchange their funny tales,
While the grass bends low and the laughter sails!

Up in the boughs, the crows compete,
For the best punchline, oh so sweet.
A tumblebug rolls, a wobbly feat,
As giggles erupt from the warm, soft feet.

Let the wind carry your worries away,
Join in the fun, it's a breezy ballet!
Laughter in nature, contagious and bright,
In the playful breeze, feel the pure light!

Revelry Among the Roots

In the subterranean, fun unfolds,
As worms tell tales that never grow old.
With giggling fungi and mushrooms in line,
They host a party, oh what a shine!

Beneath the surface, secrets abound,
With every chuckle, a new friend is found.
The soil's a stage, with roots that engage,
Each tickle of earth brings laughter to age.

Tiny beetles spin on the floor,
While ladybugs lead an encore!
Under the ground, the revelers thrive,
In the cozy dark, the joy's alive!

So dig a little deeper, find the zest,
Nature's comedy is truly the best.
In roots and humus, the laughter ignites,
In the earthy fun, find the pure delights!

The Mischief of Melodies

As the leaves play notes, a symphony so sweet,
Each rustle a rhythm, a lively beat.
The branches sway to the song of the breeze,
Tickling the air with playful tease.

The birds compose, with chirps and trills,
A melody that dances and thrills.
While the flowers sway to their heart's delight,
Under the sun, everything feels right!

A chorus of crickets joins the fun,
With laughter that sparkles, like the warm sun.
In the glade, the spirits collide,
In harmony's grip, we all take a ride.

So let's join this merry, musical spree,
With every note, wild and free.
In nature's orchestra, let's create and cheer,
For the mischief of melodies brings joy near!

Revelry in the Green

In the shade where shadows play,
Leaves wiggle, dance, and sway.
Whispered giggles in the air,
Nature's giggles everywhere.

Squirrels twirl with acorn hats,
Rabbits hop, and so do cats.
Breezes chuckle through the trees,
Tickling branches with such ease.

Sunlight dapples on the ground,
A ticklish breeze, a joyful sound.
Roots hum softly, beneath the mould,
A secret song, somehow bold.

So come, join in the wood's delight,
Where laughter echoes, pure and bright.
In every rustle, every cheer,
The forest's fun is always near.

Melodies of the Timbered Trails

Through the pathways, soft and light,
Each step brings a silly sight.
Frogs in chorus, bold and loud,
Bouncing high, a speckled crowd.

Birds crack jokes from branch to branch,
Singing songs as if to prance.
With every rustle, leaves respond,
Nature's laughter—life's great pond.

Ants on parade with tiny feet,
Marching to a rhythm sweet.
Butterflies tease with flutters fun,
Darts of color under the sun.

Joy spills forth like petals bright,
In this world, all feels just right.
The timbered trails will often find,
A melody that's sweetly kind.

Echoes of Joy in the Grove

In the grove where giggles bloom,
Fluttering sounds dispel the gloom.
Breezes toss their playful curls,
As sunlight dances, twirls and swirls.

Squirrels prance in silly games,
Whispering softly all their names.
Leaves chuckle in the light divine,
As shadows play and intertwine.

A woodpecker, a rhythmic beat,
Taps the tree with cheerful feet.
Joyful echoes rise and fall,
Nature's symphony—laughing call.

Rest a while beneath the trees,
Soak in the fun, feel the breeze.
With every rustle, magic thrives,
In the grove, where laughter lives.

Boughs That Bounce with Bliss

Up above, the branches sway,
In a happy, bouncy way.
Chirping birds share cheeky grins,
As the joyful journey begins.

Dancing leaves in soft delight,
Whisper stories through the night.
A playful wind begins its race,
Swirling gently, leaves embrace.

Sassy squirrels, wild and free,
Tumble down with glee and spree.
Nature's jesters, oh so spry,
Making mischief in the sky.

With every breeze, the laughter lifts,
In this realm where joy persists.
Boughs bounce back with playful bliss,
A hidden world we can't dismiss.

Sun-Kissed Canopies

In the shade of the tallest tree,
Whispers giggle, oh so free.
Squirrels chatter, jump and play,
Their acrobatics steal the day.

Sunbeams dance on every leaf,
Giving shadows some mischief.
Breezes tease and pull a prank,
Nature laughs, a joyful tank.

A robin winks as it takes flight,
Chasing butterflies, pure delight.
The branches sway, a merry jest,
In this canopy, we're all blessed.

Tickling branches in the air,
Echoes of joy everywhere.
Laughter rustles, life's parade,
In this green laugh, all is made.

Falling Serenades

Crimson leaves float down like dreams,
Spinning tales in sunlight beams.
Each flutter a giggle, soft and bright,
In their descent, pure comic flight.

They twirl and swirl, a funny show,
Whispering secrets only they know.
A ballet of colors, grand display,
Tickling the ground in a playful way.

Underfoot they crack and crunch,
A silly sound, a cheerful bunch.
With every step, a laugh unfolds,
Nature's humor, a joy that holds.

So let them fall, let them play,
In their dance, chase woes away.
Life's a stage, where we're entwined,
With rustling rivals, hilariously aligned.

Rustling Revelations

Whispers flit through branches high,
Rustling tales beneath the sky.
A leaf sneezes, grabs a friend,
And away they go, no need to mend.

Mice beneath a hedged embrace,
Hold a conference, quite the chase.
Who knew grass could be so sly?
As it tickles every passerby.

The wind tells jokes, in gentle tones,
As acorns topple, landing stones.
Tree trunks chuckle in broad grins,
In this giggling, green-draped din.

From roots to leaves, a comic scheme,
Together we weave, a playful dream.
Nature's humor, wide and vast,
In rustling truths, we are cast.

Echoes Through the Bark

Beneath the bark, a comedy blooms,
Saplings giggle in silent rooms.
Mushrooms bounce like silly hats,
As starlings chirp their witty chats.

Knots and grooves hold tales untold,
Like grandpa's stories, funny and old.
A woodpecker's tap, in perfect sync,
Tells of moments as toys that clink.

Through twigs and stems, a playful call,
Nature's echoes, a joyful thrall.
Every crack whispers a delight,
Awash in laughter, morning to night.

As sunlight drapes a warm embrace,
Life's a jester in this place.
With every rustle and gentle bark,
We find our joy, our joyful spark.

Vibrant Jests in the Valley

Breezes dance with silly glee,
Tickling branches, wild and free.
Whispers echo, trees will tease,
Nature's giggles through the breeze.

Squirrels chuckle, swing and sway,
In a game of hide and play.
Acorns tumble, roll around,
Laughter hidden in the sound.

Blossoms wink under bright sun,
Each petal plays, it's all in fun.
Bouncing blooms, a joyful sight,
Dancing shadows, pure delight.

Beneath the sky, so vast and blue,
The valley grins, it welcomes you.
Nature's jest, a merry sound,
In this realm, joy knows no bound.

Frolicsome Flora

Petals prance in vibrant hues,
Sharing secrets, laughs ensue.
Ferns flip-flop, caught in mirth,
Life's a carnival of earth.

Bumblebees wear tiny hats,
Buzzing jokes like chitchat chats.
Sunflowers tilt and bow with grace,
Every smile, a bright embrace.

Roots are tickling down below,
Plants tell tales, with each grow.
Gardens echo with a cheer,
Frolics happen far and near.

In the fields where colors burst,
Every leaf has jokes rehearsed.
Oh, what joy in every quirk,
Nature's humor, endless work!

The Lively Luau of Leaves

Leaves adorned like party hats,
Swinging gently, playing at.
Lively beats, the trees all sway,
Bringing joy to sunny day.

Dancing shadows, moves galore,
Happy breezes ask for more.
Raindrops tap like festive drums,
Nature's tune that tickles thumbs.

Vines entwine in playful twirl,
Every branch a cheeky swirl.
Bouncing light on each green face,
The whole grove is an embrace.

A riotous scene, the sun shines bright,
Leaves unite in pure delight.
Nature's banquet, rich and full,
Humor blooms, let laughter pull.

Raucous Rains and Revels

Pitter-patter on the ground,
Each droplet brings a jolly sound.
Rains roll in, let giggles flow,
Water dances, steals the show.

Puddles form a shiny stage,
Splashes prompt a playful rage.
Clouds above in caper suits,
Send down laughs, as nature hoots.

Raindrops glisten, sparkle wide,
Nature smiles, we join the ride.
Winds whisper jokes, trees listen in,
A wild party, let's begin!

The storm's a friend, it stirs the heart,
Making silly music, nature's art.
In each shower, joy is spun,
Life's a riot, let's have fun!

The Joyful Cascade

In the breeze, the branches sway,
Tickling cheeks in a playful way.
Silly whispers from the trees,
Dance along with giggling leaves.

Nature's jesters, swaying bright,
Tick-tock laughter, pure delight.
With every rustle, chuckles grow,
Nature's playground, putting on a show.

Under sunlight's teasing rays,
Shadows play in mischievous ways.
Sprightly murmurs, a jolly tune,
As leaves chuckle 'neath the moon.

Gusty breezes stir the cheer,
Leaving smiles and merry sneer.
In a whirl, they swiftly cling,
To the joy that seasons bring.

Nature's Cha-Ching

Leaves are clinking, cashing laughs,
In the trees, there are no drafts.
Quirky giggles fill the air,
Branches whisper, 'Life's a fair!'

Ticklish twigs, they bump and tease,
Frantic dances in the breeze.
Coins of sunlight, laughter dropped,
Nature's bank—never stopped.

Squirrels scamper, bright-eyed plays,
Poking fun in wild displays.
Underneath, the shadows play,
Mirthful antics keep gloom at bay.

Every gust, a funny song,
Twisting, turning, all day long.
Nature's riches, light as air,
Cackles echo everywhere.

Rhapsody of the Changing Shades

Colors shifting, dance of glee,
Leaves wear costumes, just like me.
Jokesters twirl in vibrant hues,
Whispers of the autumn blues.

Giggling greens to fiery golds,
Each leaf knows the secrets told.
As the winds blow, laughter spins,
Nature's game, where fun begins.

Bright marigolds and ochre winks,
In this show, even nature thinks.
Pantomimes among the branches,
In the fun, every leaf dances.

From emerald glades to rusting trees,
Celebrate with rustling breeze.
A rhapsody, light and spry,
As the world goes swirling by.

Fluttering Fables

Once a leaf found a funny friend,
Told a tale that had no end.
Fluttering high, the laughter flew,
Spreading joy as the twirls grew.

In the meadow, stories bloom,
Underneath the vast sky's room.
Every flutter writes a line,
Nature's fables, oh so fine!

Swaying gently, small tales weave,
While the wise old branches cleave.
A chirpy note, a giggle here,
Encapsulating love and cheer.

With every gust, new tales sprout,
In this world, there's never doubt.
Fables in the rustling breeze,
Nature's laughter, hearts appease.

The Leafy Laughter Lingers

Whispers in the colorful trees,
Chuckle of branches in the breeze.
Swaying in rhythm, no care in sight,
Dancing with shadows, pure delight.

Golden sunbeams play hide and seek,
Leaves flap softly, a game unique.
Giggles cascade from the rustling green,
Nature's humor, a joyous scene.

Tickles of wind coax a cheerful wiggle,
Bright green sprites that jump and jiggle.
With every flutter, laughter grows,
In this leafy world, joy overflows.

As dusk approaches, shadows conspire,
To twinkle with mirth and never tire.
Nature's own stand-up, a show so free,
Where every leaf has its own decree.

The Succulent Symphony

In gardens lush with vibrant cheer,
A symphony of colors appears.
Succulents grin with juicy pride,
Their plumpness brings joy, far and wide.

Each plump leaf, a secret to share,
Tickled by raindrops skipping in air.
Cacti jest with prickly charm,
Their jokes a sweet, amusing alarm.

Under the sun, they bask and shine,
An ensemble of green, so divine.
Harmony grows in every patch,
A playful melody, a lively match.

As colors blend in the fading light,
The symphony giggles, a pure delight.
With each soft sigh, they hum a tune,
Nature's orchestra beneath the moon.

Frothy Fronds of Fun

In a farny tangle, fronds take flight,
Frothy and full, a silly sight.
They dance with glee on a playful whim,
With every leap, their laughter's trim.

Waves of green in the cooling breeze,
Whispering secrets, if you please.
All the ferns say with each soft sway,
Join us in fun, come dance and play!

Little critters join the frolic too,
Under the fronds, in the morning dew.
A merry band with antics to spare,
Bringing joy to the fresh spring air.

With each new breeze, they tickle and tease,
Cavorting in shadows, perfectly pleased.
In this leafy realm of laughter and sun,
Every moment shared, a frothy fun.

Mischievous Breezes

A whispering wind with a cheeky grin,
Twinkling through branches, ready to spin.
With a playful tug, it ruffles the trees,
A dance of delight in the soft summer breeze.

Swaying and laughing, they play their game,
Each gust promising joy, never the same.
Chasing the leaves, a raucous parade,
Nature's own jesters, never afraid.

Over the meadows, the giggling air sails,
Tickling the flowers and telling tall tales.
As shadows grow longer, they joyfully play,
Filling our hearts with the light of the day.

With every uproar, a promise of fun,
Mischief aloft under rays of the sun.
In this whirlwind of life, carefree we glide,
On adventures of laughter, let happiness ride.

Jests in the Twilight

In twilight's glow, the shadows dance,
A squirrel twirls in a quirky prance.
The crickets hum a merry tune,
As fireflies giggle 'neath the moon.

A rabbit hops with a gentle sway,
Chasing stars that twinkle and play.
The breeze whispers jokes to the trees,
While the owls chuckle with utmost ease.

Mirth in Vibrant Mosaics

The petals blush in hues so bright,
While butterflies join in sheer delight.
Ladybugs race on a leafy track,
With tiny cheers that echo back.

The daisies sway, with jokes to share,
Winking petals in the warm air.
As colors burst, laughter combs,
Through vibrant fields, nature's homes.

Folly of the Forest Floor

A chipmunk spills his acorn stash,
As mushrooms giggle in a brash splash.
The brook babbles tales of jest,
While ants march on, never at rest.

A toad croaks with a comical flair,
As branches wave with a teasing air.
The forest floor, a stage of fun,
Where every creature plays and runs.

The Minstrels of the Maple

Crisp leaves rustle a tune so spry,
While squirrels play on branches high.
The maple sings in playful tones,
With laughter echoing through the stones.

A fox prances on a golden carpet,
Schooling shadows how to start it.
Nature's band, with whimsy rife,
Strumming joy, celebrating life.

Yonder in the Yews

In yonder grove where shadows play,
The whispers of the branches sway.
A ticklish breeze begins to tease,
As giggles float on rustling leaves.

The squirrels dance with wild delight,
Juggling acorns, what a sight!
With every leap, they seem to cheer,
As laughter sprinkles through the year.

Each twig a jester, each leaf a jest,
In nature's show, we find our rest.
The world turns bright with silly jokes,
Among the trees, the fun awokes.

Oh, join the jest, don't miss the fun,
Where yews are leaning, all are spun.
Together we'll exchange the glee,
In leafy laughter, wild and free.

The Gleaming Glade

In the glade where sunlight dips,
Frogs in bow ties do their flips.
With wild applause, the daisies cheer,
As laughter echoes, songbirds near.

The fawn stumbles in a joyful race,
Tripping over roots in a silly pace.
The meadows chuckle, swaying so bright,
In this shenanigan-filled sunlight.

A breeze of giggles, a humor spree,
Leaves rolling down with pure esprit.
A gentle nudge from the playful stream,
We dance together in this dream.

Join the frolic in the gleam,
Where nature wraps us in her theme.
With every chuckle, the world we paint,
In corners where joy has no restraint.

Tickle of the Tendrils

In tendrils curling, secrets hide,
Where ivy's giggles will abide.
A playful vine stretches with glee,
Wrapping around the tallest tree.

The blossoms blush with laughter bright,
As petals swirl in pure delight.
Bees buzz around in whimsical haste,
Chasing the breeze, no moment to waste.

Each creeping sprout boasts a jest,
In nature's laughter, we find our fest.
With twigs a-twirl and leaves bestow,
A tickle of nature in ebbs and flow.

Join the dance of tendrils sly,
Where whispers of humor never die.
With every turn of this green delight,
Let laughter blossom, radiant and bright.

Hilarity in the Harvest

In fields where pumpkins puff with pride,
A gourd in boots goes for a ride.
The scarecrow grins with straw-filled glee,
While crows crack jokes from every tree.

The corn stalks sway, they twist and twine,
As kernels giggle on the vine.
Each ear of corn has tales to tell,
Of comical times when all was well.

A basket spills with fruits and cheer,
Berries burst into laughter, oh dear!
As grapes caress with juicy twirls,
The harvest dances, twinkling squirrels.

So join the jest in fields of plenty,
In nature's bounty, life is zesty.
With every pluck, a smile we seed,
In harvest's fun, we all take heed.

The Joyous Dance of Foliage

Whirling down a sunlit street,
Leaves twirl high, a playful feat.
They caper left, then twirl right,
In the breeze, they leap with delight.

A crisp crunch underfoot, oh what fun!
In this merry dance, we're all one.
Tickling toes with each playful fall,
Nature's laughter in the autumn's call.

Gusts of wind whispering glee,
As branches sway, so wild and free.
They tease the clouds with a cheeky wink,
Inviting passersby to join and think.

When colors burst in a joyful clash,
Each leaf's giggle forms a splash.
In this grand gala, let worries cease,
For every rustle brings us peace.

Chuckles in the Changing Colors

When summer fades to a golden hue,
Leaves exchange secrets, fresh and new.
They whisper jokes to the passing breeze,
Turning drab days into playful tease.

Crimson and amber burst like cheer,
Winking at children drawing near.
With every flutter and flirty spin,
They beckon us, inviting a grin.

Jokes in the rustle, laughter in flight,
Kaleidoscope hues dance in the light.
Each color joins the jubilant band,
Creating a canvas, perfectly planned.

As nature giggles, join in the spree,
For in every flutter, there's jubilee.
Leaves shimmy and sway, a raucous show,
A festival of fun, with joy in tow.

Serenade of Shimmering Petals

Petals pirouette in the morning sun,
A ballet of blooms, oh so fun!
They laugh with the bees, sharing sweet tales,
In every rustle, the joy prevails.

Dew drops giggle as they roll and slide,
Nature's ensemble, with nothing to hide.
A petal parade, all colors unite,
Comedic moments, a pure delight.

With butterflies twirling, a humorous sight,
They dance among blooms, a laugh-filled flight.
Each petal's flutter, a comic delight,
In this flowery chaos, worries take flight.

In gardens alive with a mirthful cheer,
Nature sings boldly, for all to hear.
With petals that shimmer and quip on the way,
Join their serenade, embrace the play.

The Playful Rustle of Nature

In the heart of the woods, leaves start to chime,
With giggles and whispers, oh what a rhyme.
They rustle and shake, just like a tease,
Each sound is a jest from the trees.

Swaying branches, a jolly crew,
Creating cracks and pops, just for you.
Under this canopy, let laughter sway,
For every rustle invites us to play.

A squirrel zips by, in pursuit of a jest,
Around and around, nature's playful fest.
With every leap, there's a chuckle to share,
In this lively scene, no reason to bare.

So next time you stroll on a milling trail,
Listen closely, hear nature's tale.
For in every rustle, every breeze you find,
Lies a world of laughter, simply divine.

The Grin of Glistening Glades

In the forest where shadows play,
Branches dance in a cheeky sway.
A squirrel's leap makes the branches creak,
Tickled leaves begin to squeak.

Breezes carry a chuckling tune,
As ferns gossip under the moon.
The sunbeams wink through leafy threads,
Fluffy clouds nod above their heads.

Mushrooms giggle in a clump,
As acorns roll with a playful thump.
The brook bubbles with inside jokes,
And the owls hoot like laughing folks.

In this glade, nothing's out of place,
Each twig is part of the merry race.
Nature's jesters, oh, what a sight!
In the heart of the woods, pure delight!

Chimes of Cheer Amongst the Firs

Underneath the tall green spires,
Wind whispers in light-hearted choirs.
Dancing needles shimmer and spin,
As happy critters come tumbling in.

Cone and branch wear smiles so wide,
With secrets shared that they won't hide.
The sun peeks through as if to tease,
While shadows shimmy, shifting with ease.

Playful jays jump from bough to bough,
With silly antics, they take a bow.
Frosty pinecones giggle in glee,
Amidst the chorus of laughter's spree.

Amongst the firs, tunes never die,
With chirps and rustles, they float high.
Every moment holds a surprise,
Wrapped in joy that never denies!

Tittering Treetops at Twilight

As dusk drapes a cozy shawl,
Branches share their tales small.
Leaves shake with giggles 'round the park,
While shadows flit and revel in dark.

Hooting owls join the merry sound,
As whispers ripple around and around.
Flickering fireflies waltz above,
In this twilight, everything's in love.

Swaying trees play hide and seek,
With shrubbery chuckling, oh so sleek.
Nutty stories float on cool air,
Evidence of mischief everywhere.

Laughter bubbles as stars take flight,
In the tittering treetops at night.
What a scene, so cheeky and spry,
A canvas painted with the hug of the sky!

The Frolic of Flora

Petals twirl in a fragrant swirl,
Breezy smiles amid flowers unfurl.
Tulips tease with their vibrant hues,
While daisies chuckle, sharing the news.

Butterflies prance in playful arcs,
As bees buzz in bees' knees remarks.
In this garden, every bloom sings,
And the soil hums with secret flings.

Vines stretch out for a warm embrace,
Holding hands in a leafy race.
Sunshine dances on rosy cheeks,
While nature displays her finest streaks.

In every corner, a joyful cheer,
A festival of colors near.
The frolic of flora can't be ignored,
In this magic, laughter is stored!

Puns of the Pine

In a forest where the pine trees stand,
They joke and jest, no need for a band.
A twig snaps, laughter fills the air,
Squirrels giggle without a care.

The branches bend with whimsy bright,
Whispering jokes in the starry night.
'Needle you believe the fun we've sown?'
Pinecones chuckle, never alone.

With every breeze, a pun takes flight,
Rustling leaves in sheer delight.
The bark responds with a hearty guffaw,
Nature's jesters, with no flaw.

So let us dance beneath green skies,
Where every bough holds a sweet surprise.
In the pines, it's a giggle affair,
A merry tune fills the cool air.

Droll Leaves in Dappled Light

In the glade, the leaves conspire,
With patches of sun, they dance and tire.
A shiver and shake, a playful tease,
They wear bright masks with perfect ease.

Whispers float on gentle winds,
Leaves trade tales of silly sins.
'Did you hear what came from the brook?'
A leaf bursts forth, with laughter it shook.

When raindrops fall, they slip and slide,
A comic show, they cannot hide.
In every droplet, a joke resides,
Their whimsy spreads far, it never hides.

So join the fun, beneath twirling shade,
As nature's jesters in sunlight parade.
In dappled light, let giggles take flight,
With every movement, pure delight!

Sunshine and Sass

Golden rays tickle the grassy floor,
Where flowers smirk and the daisies roar.
'You think you're sweet, but I'm brighter still!'
The sun winks with a gleeful thrill.

With every beam, a cheeky chat,
Petals gossip like this and that.
'Who wore it best, the blooms or me?'
They laugh and boast, bright as can be.

The dandelions, so bold, so brash,
Bring sunshine sassy with every splash.
Tickled by zephyrs, they sway and preen,
In the garden, a comedic scene.

So when you wander through floral lanes,
Know the blooms indulge in playful gains.
In sunshine's glow, the sass just shines,
Nature's humor in bright designs.

The Amusement of Aerial Art

Up above, on a gentle breeze,
The kites of whimsy perform with ease.
They loop and twirl in joyous flight,
Aerial antics, pure delight.

A colorful canvas against the blue,
Each kite a tale, each tale is true.
'Look at me twist!' shouts the red and gold,
While others giggle, brave and bold.

The clouds join in, a lounge of white,
As the sun grins down, oh what a sight!
With every gust, a new joke lands,
As laughter dances through soft hands.

So raise your eyes to the skies above,
Where kites are drawn with a wink of love.
In the playful winds, laughter ignites,
In this aerial art, joy takes flight!

The Exuberance of Eden

In the garden where giggles grow,
Frolicking fruits put on a show.
The sunbeams play a merry tune,
Bouncing bright like a yellow balloon.

The flowers wiggle in the breeze,
Tickled by whispers of playful bees.
Butterflies wear their polka-dot best,
Dancing wildly, they never rest.

Juicy pears in plump delight,
Juggle with wind in a silly flight.
The playful roots tickle the ground,
Where every chuckle is joyfully found.

In this paradise filled with cheer,
Laughter mingles with each footstep near.
Nature's jesters in vibrant greens,
Chortle and cackle in clumsy scenes.

Glee in the Gnarled Boughs

Gnarled branches twist in a playful knot,
Squirrels chat in a chatterbox spot.
Their antics spark laughter and fun,
As they chase shadows beneath the sun.

Gleeful leaves rustle their secret ways,
Making jokes that brighten the days.
Each drop of dew, a snippet of glee,
Whispers of joy through the tall oak tree.

The wind swings in with a mischievous grin,
Tickling the trunks, the fun to begin.
Every branch becomes a swing set,
Where nature's creatures laugh and fret.

In the heart of the woods, there's a party alive,
Where whispers of glee but never can strive.
The gnarled boughs dance with a vibrant zest,
Bringing smiles and laughter, never a rest.

Revels of the Rustling Green

In the arms of trees, the revelry flows,
Leaves clap hands as the cool wind blows.
Frisky ferns flip and twirl about,
While the chattering creatures shout.

Grasshoppers leap with a joyful bounce,
Each melody making the flowers flounce.
Their symphony of giggles fills the glade,
Where even the shadows come out to play.

Dandelions puff with a ticklish breeze,
Sending their seeds on whimsical knees.
Each fluffy wisp a laugh let out,
Painting the air with sprightly doubt.

Underneath the canopies' cheeky sway,
Nature's jesters prepare for a play.
In rustling greens, the merry prance,
Invites us all to a light-hearted dance.

The Arboreal Antics

With arms spread wide, the trees do laugh,
In a stand-up sketch, they share a gaffe.
Each branch a story, each twig a cheer,
Bringing mischief and delight so near.

Badger and raccoon join the jest,
Playing tag in a rambunctious quest.
The shrubs giggle with a shivery sound,
As acorns tumble, rolling round.

Owls hoot jokes from their lofty perch,
Spreading chuckles in a playful lurch.
Leaves swish and swam in a comic tune,
The forest echoes a joyful boon.

With every breeze, a new prank is found,
Under the moonlight, laughter abound.
In the woods, where the funny takes flight,
Arboreal antics light up the night.

A Carnival of Color and Cheer

In the breeze, colors play,
Fluttering bright, come what may.
Squirrels dance, a comical sight,
Jumps and twirls, pure delight!

Sunlight sparkles, a giggling hue,
Leaves twirl around like a vibrant crew.
Nature's jesters, they leap and spin,
In this parade, where fun begins!

Pumpkins grin, their faces are wide,
While nearby, acorns seek a ride.
Chirping birds join in the game,
Together they laugh, none feel the same!

What a day, all frolic and glee,
Marvelous moments, wild and free.
In this carnival, joy abounds,
A festival where laughter resounds!

Exuberance Amongst the Evergreens

Evergreen whispers, tales unfold,
Laughter bubbles, and stories told.
Chipmunks chatter, quick and spry,
Dancing shadows, as time glides by.

Branches sway, in a playful tease,
Rustling softly with the breeze.
Smart little critters, their antics bright,
Igniting the woods with pure delight!

Underneath canopies, secrets shared,
Joyful moments, sung and dared.
Glistening needles catch the sun,
Echoes of merriment, everyone.

Nature's stage, where fun takes flight,
A chatterbox chorus, taking delight.
Here among giants, we laugh and play,
In the green embrace, we frolic all day!

Delight at the Forest's Edge

At the edge, where wildflowers bloom,
Happiness lifts, dispelling gloom.
Insects dance, a curious tease,
Nature's laughter floats with ease.

Colors splash in a vibrant show,
Petals flutter, basking in glow.
Breezes tickle, with jovial cheer,
Every sound whispers, "Come draw near!"

Mice scamper with a wiggle and dart,
Chasing each other, quick to start.
Sunshine filters through leafy crowns,
Painting smiles, erasing frowns.

With every rustle, the forest grins,
Inviting joy, where the fun begins.
At the edge, life bursts anew,
A playful palette in every hue!

The Joyous Bursts of Autumn

Golden leaves flutter down like chance,
Twisting, turning, a whimsical dance.
Each burst of color, a playful jest,
Nature winks, a joyful fest.

Crunchy carpets under happy feet,
Fields of laughter, oh so sweet.
Children giggle, as apples fall,
Gathering joy, they embrace it all.

Wind stirs up a playful gale,
Kites fly high, on a windswept trail.
Pumpkin patches hold a treasure trove,
With each chuckle, hearts soar and rove.

Autumn trickles laughter, like wine,
In every corner, joy aligns.
A swirl of cheer in the crisp cool air,
In nature's embrace, we find our share!

A Tapestry of Glee in Green

In the field, the grass does sway,
Tickling toes in a playful way.
Mischief dances, butterflies tease,
Nature chuckles with the breeze.

Sunlight glimmers on the pond,
Frogs leap high, of joy quite fond.
Their croaks burst forth, a silly tune,
Echoing laughter under the moon.

Squirrels dash in a dizzy race,
Chasing shadows, quickening pace.
They trip and tumble, oh what a sight!
Giggles linger from day to night.

Each leaf a jester, bright and bold,
Whispering secrets of stories untold.
Laughter weaves through branches high,
In the fabric of nature, joy will never die.

Whispers of the Wind

The wind plays tricks among the trees,
Tickling branches with gentle tease.
Leaves shake hands in a fluttery cheer,
Whispering tales that only they hear.

A squirrel chuckles and scampers fast,
Nuts dropped, oh dear! A comical blast.
Pigeons coo in a silly conga line,
Flapping wings, oh how they shine!

The sky dons clouds of puffy delight,
Casting shadows that frolic in flight.
As whispers turn into hearty roars,
Nature invites us to laugh and explore.

In every rustle, a giggle resides,
Breezes carry joy with each slide.
With a twirl of humor, the day unfolds,
As whispers of laughter break the molds.

Dance of Autumn's Palette

In autumn's breeze, the colors spin,
Leaves twirl round, a joyous din.
Golds and reds in a playful chase,
Nature's palette wears a grinning face.

Pumpkins roll, their cheeks so round,
With playful grins they bounce on ground.
Mice in scarves dart in delight,
Cheerful antics from morning to night.

Crisp air carries a laugh, a joke,
As owls wink from their leafy cloak.
Foliage giggles with rustling zest,
In this colorful dance, joy finds rest.

Frolicsome winds invite all to play,
With hush-hush giggles through autumn's sway.
Leaves flutter down, a funny display,
A circus of colors, a merry hooray!

The Giggle of the Grove

In a little grove, the sunbeams laugh,
Tickling blossoms, sharing their craft.
Bees buzz along with a merry hum,
While flowers bloom, their joy becomes.

Branches sway with playful grace,
Creating shadows that dance and chase.
Crickets chirp a rhythmic beat,
Nature's band, oh what a treat!

Breezes tease the hanging vines,
Giggling gently as sunlight shines.
A rabbit hops in a comic race,
Joyfully dashing in every space.

In this cheerful grove, spirits soar,
Leaves chuckle softly, and laughter's galore.
With every rustle, a giggle ignites,
In the heart of the grove, pure delight ignites.

Colorful Chuckles

In the breeze, the colors play,
Whispers of joy in a whimsical way.
A rustle here, a jiggle there,
Nature's humor fills the air.

Swaying branches dance with glee,
Tickling grass, oh can't you see?
Laughter echoes through the trees,
A chorus sung by playful leaves.

Dandelions puff their fluffy crowns,
While squirrels leap without a frown.
Each crackling sound brings smiles anew,
Giggles bloom in every hue.

In this park of glee and cheer,
Nature's jesters draw us near.
Colorful chuckles all around,
In leaf and laughter, joy is found.

Giggling in Golden Glades

In golden glades where giggles rise,
Sunlight winks, a fun surprise.
Leaves that shimmer, twirl, and spin,
Invite us all to join in kin.

The branches sway with carefree grins,
Where every rustle provokes spins.
The shadows dance, play tag with light,
In this mirthful, fleeting sight.

Joyful whispers fill the air,
As butterflies flit without a care.
Even the flowers nod and sway,
To the rhythm of this laughing fray.

Giggling leaves in radiant cheer,
A playful orchestra, crystal clear.
In nature's glade where laughter flows,
The beat of mirth endlessly grows.

The Joyous Jamboree

Amidst the boughs, a party thrums,
Nature's jubilee, oh how it hums!
Leaves all dancing in vibrant cheer,
As sunshine scatters laughter near.

The squirrels spin in merry rounds,
Chasing shadows, thrilling sounds.
A bash of colors, a riot of fun,
In this place where joy has run.

Each flutter and flap a festive cheer,
The trees extend their arms, sincere.
A joyous jamboree unfolds,
In this playful realm, life never gets old.

With whispers sweet, the breezes tease,
The merry rustling, a gentle breeze.
Nature's festival, pure and bright,
In every leaf, a burst of light.

Frivolous Foliage

In the woods where whimsy thrives,
Foliage dances, it comes alive.
Leaves like giggles, soft and bright,
Bringing joy to day's delight.

Branches sway in playful tease,
With subtle fonts of nature's ease.
Each leaf a smile, a chuckle free,
A symphony of glee, can't you see?

The moss below whispers a tune,
As shadows flit beneath the moon.
Frivolity in every twist,
In this green world, who could resist?

Silly breezes, teasingly bold,
Carry laughter, stories untold.
In frivolous foliage, joy's alive,
Where every leaf knows how to thrive.

Harmony in a Woodland Whirl

In a dance of twirls, branches sway,
Whispers of joy, they frolic and play.
Squirrels chuckle, chasing their tails,
While sunlight sparkles, laughter prevails.

Mushrooms giggle beneath the trees,
Tickled by arms of a teasing breeze.
Owls wink with mischief in their eyes,
And nearby, a brook gurgles with sighs.

Twirling leaves in a jesting spin,
Playful shadows where dreams begin.
The forest hums a jolly tune,
As daisies peek under the bright moon.

Nature's jesters, they bounce and glide,
In this grand theater where joys reside.
A symphony painted with cheer and glee,
In every corner, pure jubilee.

Rhapsody of Rustling Canopies

Leafy laughter in a sunlit stream,
Where branches bow, and shadows gleam.
The wind whispers jokes to passing ants,
While the daisies hum their lighthearted chants.

Breezes tease the branches high,
Sending giggles up to the sky.
A playful flicker as petals jest,
In this merry patch, all are blessed.

The sun peeks through with a playful grin,
Curious beams tangled in the din.
Mice play tag on the forest floor,
Chasing each other, laughter galore.

A chorus of cheer from the feathered throng,
Sings of splendor, a whimsical song.
In this vibrant green, joy takes flight,
Creating a world, merry and bright.

Smiles Sown with Saplings

Saplings giggle, stretching their arms,
Tickling buds with their youthful charms.
The earth chuckles underfoot, you see,
As critters scamper, wild and free.

Caterpillars wiggle with glee in the sun,
Each tiny squirm is a whimsical run.
Dancing shadows play tag on the grass,
In a fun-filled race that's sure to last.

Breezes arrive with a wild invitation,
To join in the frolic, a sweet celebration.
Mirth floats on whispers, shimmering flares,
Tickling each branch, fluffing soft hairs.

And as the day bids a bubbly adieu,
The stars blink back, a playful crew.
In this patch of wonder, hearts intertwine,
Roots tangled deep, in laughter divine.

Whimsy in the Wilderness

In a reedy breeze where merriment stirs,
Nature wears giggles, a cloak of purrs.
A sly fox grins, fumbles, and trips,
As butterflies flutter and tease with flips.

Beneath the boughs, squirrels cavort,
Juggling acorns, a funny sort.
Toadstools chuckle at the silly sight,
Where nature's antics dance through the night.

The brook babbles tales of joy and jest,
Riffing on fun like a playful quest.
Branches sway side to side in delight,
Whispering secrets till the moon's bright.

Mossy carpets cradle laughter's trace,
In this wild realm, there's always a space.
For whimsy and wonder, they freely share,
In the wilderness, joy fills the air.

Capers on the Breeze

Tiny twirls in the air,
Whispers dance without a care.
Breezes giggle, sunlight beams,
Nature joins in playful schemes.

Swaying wildly, branches move,
Giggling roots, they start to groove.
Tickled by the playful gusts,
Chaos springs from little trusts.

Sprightly shadows leap and bound,
Rustling fun, a joyful sound.
Chasing swirling shadows near,
Nature's laughter, loud and clear.

Petals flit like thoughts untamed,
Every flutter, laughter claimed.
In the gardens, mischief flows,
Life's a laugh that never slows.

Frolic of the Fronds

Fronds are flipping in delight,
Jumping jigs from morn till night.
Whirling in a green parade,
Sunlight sparkles, shadows played.

Gossamer wings skip in glee,
Nature's jesters, wild and free.
Leaves perform, a vivid show,
Spinning tales where breezes blow.

Cheeky chirps from up above,
Bouncing joy and endless love.
Every rustle, a surprise,
Hidden antics 'neath the skies.

Fronds entwine in silly dance,
Swirling in a carefree trance.
Life is comical and bright,
Joy blooms in the warm daylight.

The Kaleidoscope of Joy

Colors clash in vibrant cheer,
Waves of joy are ever near.
Swirls of laughter fill the air,
Nature's palette beyond compare.

Twirling hues in sunlit glee,
Painting smiles for all to see.
Cascades of color everywhere,
Joyful antics fill the air.

Fractal shapes in playful spins,
Every turn, the laughter wins.
A treasure chest of merry sights,
Each moment brings delight ignites.

Nature's brush, a kind of tease,
Wonders hidden in the leaves.
Life's a canvas, each day bright,
Laughter's essence, pure delight.

Laughter's Leafy Tapestry

Threads of green weave fun and cheer,
Whimsical patterns drawing near.
Each leaf sways with a quirky grin,
Telling stories from within.

Giggles echo through the trees,
Rustling whispers bring us ease.
Nature's quilt, both bright and bold,
A tapestry of tales retold.

Breezes twist and turn around,
Sprinkling joy upon the ground.
Every branch a dance, a maze,
Leafy laughter in a haze.

Underneath the laughter's art,
Joy is woven from the heart.
In this place where greens abound,
Life's grand chorus spins around.

www.ingramcontent.com/pod-product-compliance
Lightning Source LLC
Chambersburg PA
CBHW051654160426
43209CB00004B/891